Love Has No Rules

Poetic Words That Charm
Based on Love Stories with Humor

By
Charmant Kems

PublishAmerica
Baltimore

ISBN: 1-4241-7538-0
PUBLISHED BY PUBLISHAMERICA, LLLP
www.publishamerica.com
Baltimore

Printed in the United States of America

Love Has No Rules

Poetic Words That Charm
Based on Love Stories with Humor

Unique

You are unique.
I've search in the whole public.
And even in every rubric.
There is no other girl with whom I click.
No critic,
And no panic.
I'm not already trying to get in your pants, that's lunatic.
Wait don't change the topic.
Let's not do any politic.
That would be something mystic.
Or even something esoteric.
Let's be pacific and civic,
And not vague as the Atlantic.
During bad seasons climatic.
Hold on, I'm going to try to be a little more specific,
This way the comprehension would be automatic.
My love for you is gigantic.
You seduce me with your gorgeous physic.
To simply look at you makes me erotic.
Oh, girl you've transformed me from prosaic to poetic.
You hypnotize me as a beautiful music.
I believe together it'll be fantastic.
Pleasing you is my tactic.
I want to do things to you that are romantic.
I'll make you cry of joy; believe it's going to be dramatic.
I'll make sure that it's also exotic.
And I know I'm not a mechanic.
But once we're done, you'll call me, "Metallic."
Then no one would separate us, not even things that are satanic.
And that's because our love is biblical uric.

Left Alone

Have you seen her?
She is dressed in fur.
She's five feet seven.
And she looks like she came straight from heaven.
I wanted to make her my spouse.
And then buy her a house.

She has a smile that can kill,
Like those that can be seen from a hill.
She has piercing dark eyes.
With her eyes she has the power to chastise.
She has beautiful long hair.
And her beauty, to other girls is unfair.

Are you sure you haven't seen her?
Oh, I love kissing her.
I put my hands around her and kiss her passionately.
Or I simply caress her and kiss her excitedly.
She's a great kisser.
She rotates her tongue better than a mixer.

And her skin is as smooth as that of a baby.
Oh, she is so pretty.
She's sensible to my caress.
And I like that, so I never stay far from her address.
The silhouette of her body shows her splendid curves.
Her shapes are truly perfect oeuvres.

Her beauty is not artificial; it's something she was born with.
To some, such a beauty might seem as a myth.
But I know that she has many amazing part on her body.
Her body is not at all shoddy.
Like, her juicy lips are never hard or dry.
And so, I kiss them with love and let time fly.

She has a delicate neck.
Only I, have the right to touch it for a few sec.
Her chest is at a perfect 90 degrees.
When I ask her if she would like pleasure from my hands, she agrees.
I can't let anyone take her from me.
Or else I shall throw myself into the Mediterranean Sea.

"I Do"

I can't stay here for long
Alone, without you my lover along.

It's not that I'm not strong,
Or that I'm a little too young.

It's just that I want you close so I can sing you a song.

I'm not just trying to look at you in your thong.
To think so is so wrong.

And I know you understand what I'm saying because I'm not speaking in tongue.

If not, then that's too bad.
Because you are the only girl I saw in the dream I had.

You are the only girl I want in my bed.
And that's the way I want it to be till the day I'm dead.

If you believe that, you'll make me glad.

Right now without you I feel so sad.

Girl, I'm prepared to do whatever to give you the best wed.

Like, taking you to the prettiest place in Cancun,
Where we could spend our honeymoon.

We'll drink champagne while watching the moon.
I know you like laughing, so we could also watch cartoon.

And we'll make love while listening to a nice tune.

I hope we can do all that pretty soon.

I will love you for as long as I live.
Even in hard times, I'll never leave.

All that I have, to you I want to give.
And I can promise that I won't deceive.
Because I know in my love, girl you believe.

Together we could build a relationship like a house made out of bricks.
One at a time till we reach the peak.
I want you to know that you are my number one pick.
And that's not a trick.
Because with you I'm ready to take any risk.

But can I ask you something; do you like someone who licks?
And let's just I do, so you think that makes me a freak?
Because unlike the Greek I don't think it's sick.

But you got to do something for me too, if you want me to make you scream.
And you got to do it just like when you eat ice cream.

And then to relax we could go swim
Because together we make a team.

Girl, I love you, and I know we'll be together in haven.
But first let's go to church and make it happen.

And then once we are back in our room…. I'll give you the best ride.

So, can I kiss the bride?

Life

Lights out, lights in.
That's how our life has been.
Sometime dirty, sometime clean.
We sometime lose, and sometime win.
We do good, and we sometime sin.

Lights in, lights out.
We want in, and we want out.
We clock in, and clock out.
We hide in, and in the dark we come out.
We gain weight and we work out.

We love, and we hate.
We give, and we take.
We are early, and we are late.
We open the door, and we close the gate.
We are real, and we are fake.

We open, and we close.
We move, and pause.
We are humble, and we pose.
We want these, and we want those
That's the way our life goes.

Natural as a Rose

My eyes I close.
Simply to think of you my special rose.
Knowing that as natural as water flows,
Your beauty is as natural as a dove.
Now look at the stars above,
And let me know if you see a resemblance,
Because that's where your beauty belongs.

Charmed

I met this girl whose beauty makes guys freeze.
So, I approached her with ease.

I didn't want to look into her eyes,
For fear of being hypnotized

She was facing me directly.
And my heart was beating rapidly.

She must have been devilish,
For all the charms I felt her unleash

She came close to me and put her hands in my pocket,
I felt as if I were flying out in a rocket

I gave in to all of her demands.
I didn't know what was going on, I didn't understand.

But, with her beauty and splendor,
I had to give up and surrender.

Plus she promised to give me what I would ask for.
And she said she would give me even more

She asked me to put my hands around her waist,
And to give her a taste

Then she asked me to keep up the pace,
As if I were at a race.

She was saying that to motivate me
To keep me dancing until I felt free

How could I possibly say no?
When I saw her dancing techno?

That's because the way she moves drives me crazy.
Anybody would love dancing with her, even if they were lazy.

I mean she got a perfect shape.
Man, I was willing to bite on her like on a grape.

Then, she asked me if I had a girl.
I said, "No," and asked her to be my pearl.

She said, "Sure," she wants to be with me.
Then smiled and through me a key.

She said, "Tell me something to prove that you want to be my king."
I said, "Sure pretty thing."

"I want you in the present and in the future,
You don't need to change, I like your features."

She laughed and said, "Come in here my boo."

And this is all I'm telling you.

Language of Senses

We speak no language, but the language of senses.
Our senses permit us to demonstrate our love.

We don't accept separation, and we don't build fences.
We believe in the Union that was given to us from above.

We use senses to express our feeling, that's what we chose.
And this is how it goes.

I smoothly slip beautiful sounds to her ears.
She makes noises as to let me know that she's shedding pleasurable tears.

My ears pay attention to every breath she takes.
Her breathing tells how much she feels, and this is not a mistake.

I deeply look into her eyes without blinking.
Swimming deep into her eyes trying to find out what she's thinking.

She opens her eyes wider as she tries to send me a message.
I felt the passion that she was feeling in a presage.

I slowly hover my nose over her laying undressed body.
She rotates; inviting me to go all over because this is her number one hobby.

She spaciously spreads her private parts, giving me more room.
I delicately get there and sense her natural perfume.

I neatly put my lips on her forehead for a little kiss.
She wets her lips, requesting me toward them to give her bliss.

She puts her lips back into her mouth, and looks down onto her chest.
I understood where she wanted me to go, so she smiles as she crests.

I start sliding my hands on her pretty skin.
She trembles as if she was electrocuted from her toes to her chin.

She then opens her mouth and glides her tongue over her luscious lips.
She wants to French kiss, so we kiss, while I have my hands on her hips.

Now she expresses what she feels with a big smile.
Her eyes look straight at me, as she gazes with style.

Shy as she is, and not being able to stop smiling while looking at me, she puts on a hood.
Her eyes have said more than what her words could.

Suicide

"Dear wife, we used to be great lovers.
We used to be deeply in love with one another.
We used to make love for hours,
And then share wine and bread.
But for a while now you have been rejecting me.
I don't know what went wrong.
You don't want to tell me anything.
You have turned your back at me in bed,
And you have been treating me as if I were the Judas in the Bible.
That makes me think that there must then be a christ, since it's not me.
Tell me, or show me who he is by giving him a kiss on the lips.
So that I can beg him for mercy,
And ask for forgiveness for a sin that I did not commit.
Unless loving you is the sin.
If it is, then guilty I am.
Should I then be put on a cross?
Well, my Lord has already done that for me,
And for that I'm grateful.
Should I then hang myself like Judas did?
Or maybe I've already been hanged the day you stopped loving me."

Deeply Tender

You are, as tender as my hands touching your body,
    As tender as my eyes admiring your beauty,

    As tender as the softness of your delicious lips,
    As tender as you giving me a kiss,

    As tender as the shapeliness of your waist and thighs,
    As tender as the reflection of your face on my eyes,

    As tender as our eyes meeting in the dark,
    As tender as your curves, more curvy then the St. Louis ark,

    As tender as your face shinning like a star,
    As tender as your perceptible beauty from afar,

    As tender as your nice scent like the rose's perfume,
    As tender as the elegance of a sun's loom.

Let me feel you sensual tenderness.

I'm There with You and Here for You

I can't accept letting you go through this by yourself, for your misery makes me miserable as well. So hear what I have to say.

Every time he won't be there to talk, I'll be there to listen.

When he won't have time for you, I'll spent time with you.

If he holds you by the hand, I'll hold you by your waist.

If he won't hold the door for you, I'll open mine to you.

Whenever he won't take you out, I'll escape with you to a place where we can be alone.

If he kisses you on the lips, I would kiss you on your neck, on your chest and all over your beautiful body.

When he won't touch you, I'll gently lay my hands on you and caress you.

Whenever he won't sleep with you at home, I'll spend the night with you and I'll spend it making love to you.

If he ever tries to put his hands on you, I'll throw a fist at him.

If he won't defend you, I'll protect you, I'll always be by your side.

If he won't offer you anything, I'll provide everything you need.

If he won't trust you, I'll believe in you and in everything you do.

I'm not simply jealous, but I also envy what he has in you, for in you I see great treasure.

If ever he throws you out of his house, I'll throw roses on the floor as I welcome you home.

When you feel alone and need a companion, know that you got a friend in me.

And when you need intimacy, for someone to hold, remember you got a lover in me.

You may belong to him, but your heart belongs to me, as my whole belongs to you.

Have my love and hold my heart, let me have all you got to offer. I'll hold you in my arms, and your love in my heart, and that shall last forever.

Je T'Aime

I want to tell you "je t'aime."
One on one we'll be like the letter M.
That way you'll truly know who I am.
I'll tell you more in the pm.

All this is to show you that you are my miss.
Let me tell you, I really want to give you a kiss.
I'll make all your worries cease.
You'll feel nothing but peace.
Like the flow of the wind in Greece.

But please, don't give me a quiz.
Unless it is to satisfy you because that I can do with ease.
I can't tell you how, but I can show you, that's just the way it is.
For that I will need to get to your room, so I need your keys.
Then you'll find out why some call me, "the whiz."
You can be sure we'll make great memories.

Eh! Do you remember that day you told me you had a dream?
And that, in the dream I made you scream
because I had you rolling as a nice shiny rim.
I'm kidding, but as a pervert, that's what I may seem.
Trust me, I'm as sweat as ice cream.

But tell me, am I dreaming or is this real?
Maybe I'm not thinking clearly because I missed a meal.
But if this is real, we got to make a deal.
I mean, I love your personality plus you got that look that can kill.
Yeah, I'm ready for anything, and trust me I got the will.
I know I might sound crazy, but don't worry. I'm not ill.
What's killing me now though is your sex appeal.

I can feel it coming from across the room.
If it gets any closer, we could kiss goodbye to the roof.
Then do it as we want, because there is no rule.
And once you start feeling my energy, don't be surprised, I get it from my roots.
Scream as loud as you want, and ask for anything, I won't think that you are rude.

As long as we're both in the mood,
We can do it anywhere; we don't even have to be nude.
At the library behind the books, I bet we could.
At night on the warm sand at the beach, we won't get booed.
In the living room, on the couch or by the fireplace, that would be good.
In the kitchen, by the sink or on the table, I think we should.
In the laundry room by the warm running dryer, I know we would.

All we got to do is keeping it clean.
So far that's the way it has been.
That's because I 'm not a teen.
And let me tell you, you are the best I've seen.
I'm not talking about sex, I'm talking about…Well, you know what I mean.
Now you are officially my queen.

The Burden of Love

If I were to die,
And that the undertaker finds my casket to be too heavy,
Explain to him that it is because of all the Love that my heart still carries
for you.

But my Love,
I am not dead yet
And there are many things that I would like to do with you.

So, I ask you to hold my hand and listen to my heart
For my heart has deeply fallen in love with you.

Happy Birthday

Blues skies open up,
And give space to the shining red sun.

Full moon shines in blue color
Covering the entire earth's surface.

These are only two of the things
that happen every time you smile.

But that does not surprise me,
I'm only amazed by the way your beauty
keeps growing as the years go by.
Happy birthday.

The Girl on the Second Floor

I was walking by the garden.
Then a reflection of the sun hit me all of a sudden.
A pretty girl was standing there, opening her window.
In her hands she was holding a pink pillow.
The pillow matched her pinkish lips.
I was already imagining Titanic type of love affair but on different ships.

I looked at her for a few sec, but then I could no longer see her.
This to me was an act of terror.
The sun was shining directly to my eyes.
I was hoping that it was going to go under the skies.
I stood there and kept looking.
I don't know what I was thinking.

But I knew what the sun was doing was unfair.
Tears were falling from my eyes trying to see this beauty that was rare.
I was wishing for our lips to meet each other's.
And share a passionate kiss as that of a baby and his/her mother.
Then, all of my distress went away when I heard her say, "Come over."
That was the best think I heard that day, so I went closer.

She then said, "You must be the handsome prince charming I've been
waiting for."
I was hastily thinking of what to reply to get a big score.
I quickly wiped the tears the sun had made me shed.
I said something, but she didn't hear me so she asked, "You said?"
I was going to repeat what I said, but this time at a different pace.
I said, "You are so sweet, that tells me that your heart is as beautiful as
your face."

She smiled and then walked away.
I was a little worried, but I knew there was no reason to go astray.
Then she came back and asked, "Aren't you going to ask for my number?"
I said, "Sure, if I get your number, I'll surely call you before the end of
September."
She laughed and said, "Today is the last day of September."
I said, "That's right, so I better remember."

She then threw a paper plane out the window and it landed in from of my feet.
Inside she had her phone number and she had stamped her kiss at the
back of the sheet.
I asked her to come down and come close.
I picked up and was holding in my hand a white rose.
She came down took the rose, and kissed me on the chick.
But then she ran back up pretty quick.

I asked her why she was running for.
She ignored what I'd asked, and she was smiling from the second floor.
Today, she's the one I adore.
And our type of love has never been seen before.

A Walk Through the Park

"Excuse me; can I get your autograph? Sign it to Frank Kerry.
Oh, I'm sorry I thought you were Beyonce, but you look more like Hally Berry.
I hope you don't think that I met to insult you.
Because, it's obvious that you look better than her, yes you do.
Can I still get your autograph though, since you've proven me wrong?
I used to think Beyonce was the most attractive girl since the day I saw her
in a thong."

"May I have the honor of knowing your name, or should I call you, 'Beautiful?'
I know that this is kind of weird but truss me, I'm not a fool.
You are so pretty, the first thing I noticed about you was your lips.
Okay, that's not totally true; I was actually looking at your hips.
But I really think that you got great lips and pretty eyes.
I know, I sound like every other guy, but unlike them, I'm not telling you lies."

"I'm already learning about you, I can tell you three things that I know."
She finally talked, "You just met me, what can you really know?"
"Well, I can tell that you are gorgeous, intelligent, but also sad.
I can add that a man in your life is making you unhappy, and he's not your dad."
She replied, "You think you know everything, don't you?"
"I don't know everything, but I know this is true, and I think you do too."

"I think you got really nice boobs, sorry, I met to say nice loods.
That's not a word, see you got me confused because of your goods.
So, what are you doing in the park this late, you know it's dangerous?
Criminals, when they see sexy ladies like yourself they are never generous."
She answered, "I'm waiting on my boyfriend."
"Boyfriend! This late! Sorry but I think he found another girlfriend."

"I bet he knows that he's lucky, and therefore treats you like a queen.
I bet he takes you to places where you haven't been."
She said, "I think he treats me just fine."
"Hesitation! Ha ha! That's never a good sign.
Then, why does he leave you here in the dark by yourself?
You think he cares about you, but I think he cares only about himself."

"Are you sure he takes good care of you the way I would?"
She answered, "He's a good guy, and he just sometime has too many rules."
"Good guy maybe, but he is not taking care of business.
I think he does not have time for you because of his selfishness.
You know what, let's go to a warmer place, let's go to a restaurant.
After that, maybe we'll go over my place, and by the way I don't rent."

I didn't want to be rude so I left my phone number on the bench.
That was in case her ex-boyfriend wanted to know where she went.

Last Chance

I know what's making my heart so fragile
I used to digest her love until full.
This girl used to be my loving angel.
I remember her being so beautiful.
Why did not she give me another glance?
She decided to put my heart in chains.
And all I wanted was a second chance,
But all that was given to me was pain.
I wish that she could have given me love.
What can I do to get her next to me?
I could have sworn with my hand on a stove.
And show her that I'm not her enemy.
What is there to do before she is gone?
Or maybe I should accept that I'm done.

Tender, You Are

More tender than the flow of the wind through a herd
  I want your tenderness.
More tender than the feather of a newborn bird.
  I want to feel your tenderness.

More tender than full moon in the middle of summer.
  I want to see your tenderness.
More tender than the love of a baby boy for her mother.
  I want to have your tenderness.

More tender than the first snow falling from the sky.
  I want to crab your tenderness.
More tender than the sweet taste of a warm apple pie.
  I want a taste of your tenderness.

More tender than the tip of a nose.
  I want to touch your tenderness.
More tender than the softness of a rose.
  I want to smell your tenderness.

My Lucky Day?

One morning, I was introduced to a pretty girl, so I invited her to lunch.
We decided to meet at twelve to grab a munch
I brought a poem with me that I wrote on human relations
We sat at a restaurant and started our little conversation
After a few minutes, I gave her the poem and ask her to read it loudly.
She started with the title, "Forget About The Poem, Kiss Me Instantly."

So I leaned toward her and kissed her, and I did it pretty well.
She looked surprised and asked, "What does S.L.A.P.M.E spells?"
I reflected for a second, and I said, "Sla.. Slap me!"
I then told myself, "Maybe she was trying to get back at me."
It was too late. She did it so hard that I was disoriented for a minute.
With a smile she said, "That's my way of letting you know that you are cute."

We chatted for a little longer, and then we left in different directions.
I told her I was going to call her so I could tell her about my affections.
With a sarcastic tone she said, "I'll be waiting for your call sir."
So later in the evening, I called her.
"Hey Chrystal, how are you doing, this is Steve."
She asked, "What do you tell someone right before you leave?"

I wondered why she asked, but I answered, "You tell them bye."
Then I heard no sound but the phone tone right when I was to ask her, "Why?"
"Hello, hello!" I then realized that she had hung up.
I called her back, wondering why she was acting up.
I asked, "What do you say to someone you like and really care for too?"
She said, "Well I simply say, I love you."

"I love you too Chrystal," I replied.
She said, "Not bad, you must think that you are fly."
I said, "Yes I do, but can I ask you something personal?"
She said, "Sure, I'm open, plus nothing is too personal."
I said, "Okay. How old are you and how much to you weigh?"
I added, "That's because you look bad, of course that's in a good way."

"Old enough to be legal and weigh just enough for you to handle."
I said, "Well, well. I better get some candles."
Then I heard a voice ask, "Mom, what are you doing on my phone?"
I was confused, so I hung up pretty quick and I was gone.
After that, for a week I did not call her anymore.
And once I did, I never admitted ever calling her before.

Undress

Let me undress you with my eyes.

Your dress doesn't seem to be able to hide your shapes.

As I look deeply into your dress I see your thighs.

They look as delicious as your lips that taste like grapes.

But I can't stop looking at your face.

And your eyes pierce into my skin and overtake my mind.

You can't be human; you must be of a different race.

And I would want to become a deer if you were a beautiful hind.

Oh, I wish I had the power to pierce deep into your heart.

But, now I'm getting lost in my desire.

But, I don't want this feeling to depart.

I would accept to be your lover and never retire.

I must admit that my eyes are not strong enough to undress your rich body.

But I know that a simple touch of my hands would unleash on you great pleasure.

My hands would float on your body with the rhythm of a nice melody.

And my hands would love doing just that; they think you are more than a treasure.

And now I close my eyes and concentrate on the rhythm of my touch.

This I shall do until I feel you really clutch.

The Glance That Started It All

As I glanced! I saw your splendor.
As I looked! I saw your shape.
As I stared! I saw your beauty.

As I talked! I felt your charm.
As I spoke! I felt your intelligence.
As I chatted! I felt your confidence.

As I concentrated! I sensed your perfume.
As I dreamed! I sensed you presence.
As I reflected! I sensed your passion.

As I thought! I acknowledged your charisma.
As I listened! I acknowledged your humor.
As I analyzed! I acknowledged you gorgeousness.

Now that I'm observing.
    I'm seeing your elegance.
    I'm appreciating your presence.
    I'm admiring your intelligence.

And every time that I dream or think of you, I feel you next to me.

My Lost Lover

A lost time took my love away from me.
In my heart was a nice feeling leaving.
My own time had become my enemy.
Deep inside I still wanted some loving.
When my lover was about to be gone,
My heart started getting a bit weaker.
I decided to make myself go on.
I almost went as wild as a streaker.
Asked myself questions like a worried wife.
Who here can help me get my lover back?
I had to make changes in my own life.
So I carried my pain on my strong back.
My love had to be back in my life soon.
Or never more my eyes would see full moon.

Girl, Let Me Read to You

"You are everything and better.
As long as I got you with me, other things don't matter.
I know you'll never let me fall in the gutter.
When you were far from me it felt cold as in the winter.
But now I got you, so I guess that makes me a winner.

What I say might sound funny.
But let me tell you something honey.
And I'm not saying this because I feel horny.
I've been in love with you from the day you kissed me.
That day, I was jumping like a happy bunny.
I remember it was a beautiful afternoon, and it was sunny.

You were walking toward me with a pretty smile,
That smile that can be seen from a mile.
You looked as beautiful as an Egyptian girl walking by the Nile.
You looked so good; I thought I was dreaming for a while.

And I admire you because unlike other girls you don't just take.
That's because you are not fake.
Girl, you know what, let me make you a cake.
But you disserve so much more; so let me take you to the lake.
And make love to you and give you an earthquake.

I'll have my hands on your waist and you won't escape.
I'm not an animal, and definitely not an ape.
But I can be your batman in bed, even though I got no cape.
And if you like, we could make our own private tape.

I'm just kidding, but one day though I'll take you on a private jet.
I've been dreaming of doing this from the first day we met.
In the jet, we'll do different things that we haven't done yet.
I'll get you wet.
And we'll do different sets.
I don't want to make a bet.
But everything you dream of, that day you'll get.

I'll do things to you and then we'll talk about it on the phone.
I hope you don't think that I'm cheesy because I'm just telling the truth
to my hon.
I need you more than I need light from the sun.
I won't give up on you even if they try to shoot me with a gun.
Because being with you is so fun.

I love you so much, and want to be there to provide.
My heart is opened to you so wide.
Therefore, you'll never need to hide,
As long as you got me by your side."

Love to the Woman

I look at you and understand why I would be willing to give so much love to a woman.

But you are not just a woman, you are the woman.

The woman that I dream of loving whose heart is full of affection.

Her eyes have melted the oceans of ice that have lived in my heart.

Whose presence changes the normal biting of my heart and gives it the rhythm of an African tam-tam.

Yes, I'm talking about you, my lady in silk.

You with the appealing smile which charms me like a flute does to a serpent.

Hypnotized, I may be, and if I am, it is willingly.

Yes, I dare looking deep into your eyes.

Because every time our eyes meet, it's as if I see the sun rise.

The sun truly recognizes your beauty and so does the wind.

Proof of it being that at your presence I feel as if I was lifted off the ground and pushed toward you by the wind.

Forgive me if I can't find words to describe what I feel for you and your incredible elegance.

The reason is language was not made to express or even describe such mysteries.

But with a simple touch of our lips. Oh, those arrogant lips of yours, juicy and full of taste.

A simple kiss on them would express all the feelings I have for you.

You are a beauty that no one dares criticize for there is no foundation.

A beauty that makes many people question the fairness of humanity.

Even philosophers don't seem to comprehend this beauty.

Historians and geographers have declared you the first wonder of the world.

You know, people fear staring at you for fear of going insane.

I'm also afraid of approaching you, so I write this letter.

I can't stop thinking about your face, your eyes. Them small eyes but yet full of life.

My lady, if I may ask you to look up in the skies because roses are falling and so am I for you.

If you won't give yourself to me, at least give me your beautiful heart.

I'm not sure that angels exist on earth, but I'm sure that is they do,

They would have a hard time measuring up to your beauty.

For your love or a kiss of your lips is worth more then a thousand kisses from an angel.

Goodbye

Don't look back,
if it is to say goodbye,
or you'll see tears falling from my eyes,
those eyes that deeply desire to see you smile.

Don't give me hope,
if you are to break my heart.
For my heart dearly desires to Love you.

Don't touch my lips
If you won't be kissing them tomorrow.
For your kiss is what nourishes me.

Don't hold my hands,
If you won't let me hold you next to me.
For my hands don't want to hold another woman but you.

Don't tell me you care about me,
If you won't let me take care of you.
For in my life, you're the one I care the most about.

Don't, please don't, I beg you

Don't tell me that I'll be alright,
If you won't be here next to me.
For I simply can't live without you by my side.

If You Want Me

If you want me, don't follow me but walk with me.
    And I won't come home late to you; I'll even surprise you.

Don't leave me, but stay with me.
    And I won't go out without you, I'll stay home alone with you.

Don't offend me, but encourage me.
    And I won't insult you; I'll speak beautiful words to you

Don't slap me, but massage me.
    And I won't hit you; I'll sensually caress you.

Don't bite me, but kiss me.
    And I won't hurt you; I'll have my hands everywhere on you.

Don't simply sleep with me, but make love to me.
    And I won't only make love to you, I'll fully satisfy you.

Don't cheat on me, but have sex with me.
    And I won't quit on you, I'll overwhelmingly please you.

As you want me, you are mine and I am yours.

Close to My Heart

Far you are, but close to my heart.

You are all that I have, and all that I want to possess.

My heart has no home, and it finds refuge in you.

You are the only, who though far, is more present than all others.

Though far, you are more present in my thoughts.

And in my thoughts, I feel your heat,

The heat of your chest, and only your chest I want against mine.

Far you are, I feel the softness of your lips, and only your lips I want to kiss.

Far you are, I feel the tenderness of your waist, and only on you I want to lay.

Though far I know that you are with me.

I want you when I'm happy, because you are the one who makes me happy.

I want you when I'm sad because you are the only one who can put a smile on my face even when I'm miserable.

I love you, and I love loving you.

I wait, and I'll always wait for the day we'll be together.

That day is already in my thoughts.

That day is already in my dreams.

You and only you in that room facing me.

No light, but the reflection of your beauty.

No heat but the one coming off your nicked body.

We are letting our imagination guide us.

And I'm showing you how much I love you.

I'm proving my love to you.

And you are letting your feelings out as you are accepting my love.

I love you.

I love you not only for your beauty,

Even thought that beauty can make blind.

I love you not just for the softness of your lips,

That softness that can paralyze.

I love you not simply for the heat of your body,

That heat that can burn.

I love you for who you are, spiritually, physically, mentally and emotionally.

I want you the way you are and I want you for the rest of my life.

I love you.

Hello!

Hello! Have we met?
Oh, I'm sorry I guess we haven't met yet.

Forgive me for approaching you this way.
I'm Chris, for Christopher by the way.

And you are, mademoiselle?
Oh, I guess I will then call you, "Belle,"
Since you won't come out of your shell.

May I say that you look familiar?
And please don't think that I'm a liar.

But I really believe we've met before.
Please, let me get the door.

As I was saying, I believe we've met some place else.
Pardon! Oh, you believe this is false.

Then how do you explain that I know you like dark chocolate.
Oh, you think I was guessing, let's see if this time you'll find an outlet.

You love flowers and the blue ones even better.
You sleep with silky pajamas, and when cold you sleep with your sweater.

I believe that's because you got tender skin.
You love to be kissed on your chin.

You don't like too much make-ups, you like your face to be clean.
And please cheer up, you got the prettiest face I've seen.

Oh, you think I'm a good flatterer! I'll take it as a compliment.
Don't be so defensive, I'm not trying to start an argument.

You look very nice by the way, and you have a nice scent.
My guess is that you are from Paris because of your nice accent.

I'm English, you are French. Well, all the fights are history.
You still haven't told me your name, maybe you want to be a mystery.

I'll be honored if you would accept to have dinner with me.
And don't worry, I'm not about to embarrass you by getting on one knee.

I know a nice place where they serve French cuisine.
I used to go there with a friend when I was a marine.

Thanks! Well, Clementine. I think that's a pretty name.
I know it's hard on you ladies the way most men behave. It's a shame.

But, there are still some of us who know how to be a gentleman.
I only want to get to know you, and that's my only plan.

Don't Leave Me

Christina, I'm sorry but I just can't do it.
I mean, even if I wanted to let you go,
My heart would still be holding unto you.

You know, my mom used to tell me
That the most beautiful thing on the earth
Was the trees.
But see, mom never saw you.
She does not know that you are
The most beautiful flower of the blue color ones.
She does not know that the most beautiful love song
Was written for you.
And that the most romantic poem
Was written about you.

Me, on the other hand always knew that you were
The most beautiful thing on the earth from the day I saw you.
When I saw you, I said to myself, "I never knew that angels could fly this low."
And my heart has been holding onto your wings since that day.

Forgiveness

Maybe I've done you wrong, well I take that back. I know I have done you wrong. I've caused you great pain without even realizing it. But now I understand that every time I hurt you once, I hurt myself twice because you are twice as much important to me than I am to myself. I really care about your feelings, and I wish that I could be the one to console you.

You know, I once read that most blind men, when asked what they would choose to see if they were given the opportunity to see for one minute, most would choose to see the light of the day. I thought about it for a second, and then asked myself what I would have chosen if I was in that situation. The choice was clear to me; I would have chosen to see your face because you are the light that shines in my life. I'm sorry.

Dying Rose

Your rose has been dying, did you notice?
Have you stopped loving me?
Or am I simply lost in my own confusion?
The truth is you never started loving me.
For love never dies and never ceases.

Tell me that I'm wrong.
And I'm saying this with hope,
With the hope that you still carry love for me.
For I don't know how I shall walk without your love.
Maybe I'll walk as a blind man in a dessert looking for water.
But even a blind man has a better chance of finding water,
Than me finding my steps without you by my side.

How daring am I to compare you to water.
Your love is truly worth more then all the oceans put together.
A simple kiss from you leaves a scrumptious taste in my mouth for days.
So much that other things don't have a taste anymore.

My desires to always be with you are great.
So immense that even in my dreams I don't crave other ladies.

I've been crying lately, but with no tears.
For all the tears went down to my heart, trying to keep it from drying out.
For my heart has experienced a drought from your love Adriana.
I hope I'm wrong.
I should die, but never stop loving you.
I know I will die, but love shall be mine, and love never dies.
Therefore with love we shall everlastingly live, if you love me.

You know, the things we have done together has showed me that love truly exist.

But I wonder if it's simply a gift, or a treasure that we all seek.

A treasure that only few are fortunate to find and hold,

I don't know how much longer I'll be holding mine.

Adriana, my love for you is real, as real as the skies are blue,

Unless the skies are green, then my love for you has fallen to the sea.

But, red is the color of my love for you.

For my heart is red, as red as the blood that runs trough your veins.

For weeks now my heart has stopped biting.

But my love for you has kept me going.

Maybe I'm already dead, and I'm now living in this love that brings eternity.

For my heart has no life, unless you live next to me Adriana.

Only a touch from your lips can assure me of this life.

Or I will simply put a knife through my heart to end this misery.

Oh oh, Was I dreaming?

Adriana, is this you? Wake up!

Was I dreaming, was I dead?

Oh Adriana, you must have kissed me!

I should have never doubted your love for me.

I will everlastingly love you, and we shall undyingly be together.

On the Train

I was on my way to Chicago, and I almost missed the train
I was fortunate because it started to rain
There were only two empty seats, and both were facing a pretty lady
Unfortunately for me she had next to her, her baby
Not an enfant, but a fully grown man.
And not your average dude either, he was more like 6'10"

Every time his eyes and mine met, I quickly looked away.
But I wanted to talk to the lady, so I just had to find a way.
That must have been my lucky day for soon the giant was asleep.
Now I'm thinking, "This is that type of girl everyone would like to keep."
So, I looked toward her and asked, "Do you want to hear something funny?"
With a smile she said, "Sure, as long as you are not making fun of my honey."

I said, "Of course no one wants to do that, unless you want your butt kicked."
Smiling she said, "Don't worry, he's a gently giant, you are not at risk."
I then asked for her number so that I could text message the joke.
Then I saw Tarzan moving, scared me to the point that I spilled my coke.
She was laughing, so I said, "What's this, beauty and the beast?"
I heard a voice say, "Who you calling the beast, would you like to meet my fist?"

I said, "I'm sorry sir, but you are not who I was talking about."
I then sent her the text, and I was waiting for the next stop to step out.
She was laughing while I was about to have a heart attack.
I soon calmed myself down after she text messaged me back.
It said, "Don't mind him; he thinks that he's so tough."
I text messaged back, "Well, he must be, since he looks so buff."

She then asked, "Tell me, how they call you?"
She carried on, "I feel like I know you, this feels like déjà vu."
I said, "Well maybe we've met, I'm Romeo, and you must be Juliet."
I continued, "Talking to you right now feels like playing the Russian Roulette."
She laughed so hard and said, "Let's go to the dinning cart so we could chat."
I said, "Sure, as long as Hercules doesn't follow me with a bat."

I then asked, "Why don't you date someone of your own size?"
I carried on, "I'm not telling you what to do, that's just what I would advise."
She said, "Well, don't worry about him, that's my younger brother."
I asked, "Younger, and that big, and just how big is your father?"
She replied by saying, "Shut up and kiss me, you ask too many questions."
I said, "I must admit, that's a very good suggestion."

Well, that's all I'm telling, you can figure out the rest.
By the way, if you still want to know what the joke said, here it is:
"You are beautiful, you remind me of someone, my grand mom, only she
got a better body."

Not Shallow

You are pretty in the eyes of few men.
You deserve a king who has no kingdom.
"You have a pretty face," said the blind man.
A face like yours should never see freedom.
You look better when away from the light.
You and cute don't belong in one sentence.
I think it's clear why that would not be right.
Plus that could get us to the death sentence.
You love me but on my side, not the same
The more clothes you wear the better you look.
I love when you dance, even though you're lame.
Nothing taste bitter than the food you cook.
You should know by now that I'm not shallow.
I stay while other run from your shadow.

Guide Me

I've looked everywhere for girls who resemble you. But every time I find one who comes close to your beauty, I realize that she doesn't have your charm or your character. Every time I come close to one who comes close to having your sense of humor, I realize that she doesn't have your glamour or your aspect. And every time I find one who comes close to your personality, I realize that she doesn't have your elegance or your charisma. Now I don't know where to look anymore. My heart and eyes that you blinded can't find their way anymore. Only you can guide my heart. Come guide me toward your love.

Her Description

Where did she go? She was just on my right.
Please, I beg, someone switch on the light.
Our lips were just touching, tell me I wasn't dreaming.
Oh! Goodness! I hope she's not far and that she's coming.
Someone please help me find her.
Or, missing her would kill me like a cancer.
She's a beauty standing tall at 5' 9,"
A Beauty that keeps all the boys in line.
Sexy shinning lips that are with no doubt tender,
And for those lips, who wouldn't be willing to surrender.

Her dressing is impeccably stylish.
No, she's an African black pearl with the charm of an Irish.
No question about that, her body is in perfect shape.
Yes, she has the rare type of beauty that deserves to be put on tape.
Her beauty should never, in no case be evaluated
Because there is fear of making other girls jealous if she was ever rated.
And don't think that she got no brain
Because she would outsmart you with the right answers, she's usually the first in lane.

She loves dancing, she has no preference for a man dancing like an African or an American, to her it's all the same.
Her only reference is that the man can actually dance and that he's not lame.

If you ever kept watching her dancing, there is chance of going insane.
She would have you staring at her and forgetting that you were standing in the rain.

If you wanted to see her, you should prepare yourself for a shock.
Believe me, you will question the beauty of other girls you've seen like I
did, even though I'm hard like a rock.

Her face would get you lost in her world.
You will then speak of nothing else but beautiful words.
I think one of her many great attributes are her eyes.
Oh man, those spellbinding eyes, and I'm not even going to talk about her
thighs.

Her chest, well, I won't go into details, but they are perfectly shaped like
a bird's nest.
Her irresistible beauty should never be questioned, and her presence
would put any doubt at rest.

Loosing her would be loosing my most precious part and therefore
making me worthless
Because, without my heart I will not last, I will soon go breathless.

Dream Girl

"Are you the girl from my dreams?
If you are, let me say that you are unbelievable.
Your legs are silky and firm.
Am I still dreaming or am I loosing my mind?
You know that I got a girl in my real life, don't you?
But I guess it's not considered cheating since this is a dream.
Lets then finish what we started.
This feels so real, I'm liking it
Can we do this again some other time?
Let me try this, so this is what they call missionary.
But, are you sure that I'm dreaming?
This feels as good as when I was cheating
This is the best dream I've ever had."
Then I heard someone knocking at the door
I said, "Who's there, I'm trying to sleep?"
I continued, "I'm not waking up or stopping, you better believe that."

Then I heard her ask, "Sean, are you cheating on me?"
I said, "No this does not count, this is only a dream."
She asked, "What dream?" She walked in and slapped me.
I tell you, I knew then that I wasn't dreaming.
As you can see I was the victim in this situation.
I was mislead and abused by that girl.
I hope this never happens to anyone else but to me, again and again.

Marriage Proposals

"You know, if men lived on Mars and Women on Jupiter, I would have built a bridge across to come ask you to marry me. And if I could fly, I would take you right now on my wings and take you to heaven and then ask you to marry me. But since we are both on earth and I clearly can't fly, would you marry me?"

"You may know that Mary loves berries, I mean she lives in this fairy tale. So, for their anniversary with Terry, I bought her all types of berries, I mean strawberries, blueberries, and Jerry even bought her cherries and other things from the prairie, anyway, would you marry me?"

"My love, I haven't been the best I could be. I've caused you a lot of grief, and I haven't been spending a lot of time with you. But, today I'm bringing to the table a solution to that problem. You know how many men complain about their marriage, about how happy they were before marriage and then marriage changed all that and made them miserable? Well, I think that is time for me to be miserable, so would you marry me?"

I Believe in America

As eagles wing high above the Majestic Mountains covered with snow
And buffaloes gather in the garden valleys where beauty is no stranger
I stand in the middle of this heaven where the laws of Moses govern

Who shall dare cast a stone onto this nation, would dare God Himself.
For this is a nation with colors of the rainbow that stood above Noah's
new world
And, with open heart, all are welcomed like the Jewish were in Israel
after the genocide

Our Nation has inherited liberty from our founding fathers and those
who stood by them
A gift that numerous people of the world would willingly and gladly
shed blood for
A treasure that each one of us must swear to protect till our very last breath

In America, with every sun rise, comes new hope
A new chance to life, a chance to rise
Therefore, I believe in America

Love with Faith

If you were a rose,
And if my love for you could grow a rose,

My heart would have been a garden full of you.

Yes you, the lady dressed in white silk
Whose skin has the taste of light milk.

I observe you like a panther does his prey.
Hopping to get real close to you, and this I pray,
At bay, staring at your lips that I would love to kiss, if I may.

But, I can't approach you and your pretty eyes just yet.
Even though I feel like we've already met.

It's true that you look good in white, but even better in red.
And in my dreams I see you in these colors the day of our wed.

No, I'm not loosing my mind; I'm simply passionate about you.

Okay, I realize that I don't know much, but I do know one thing.
One thing about you that makes you perfect, "EVERYTHING."

Sure, I realize that I'm a little bit too direct.
But I won't go too far because I own you some respect.

I hope you understand that I'm letting my emotions out.
Well, that is something you can think about.

To you, I have a lot of love to give.
But, this gift, I must also receive.

And for you I would be willing to take the cross.
For your death to me would be a greater loss.

What do I want? My goal is to one day get you a ring
Because with you as my queen, I'll be happier than a king.

And I'll be envied even by the bourgeois.
I want to love you as you please because in love there is no law.

Maybe I'm wrong, but one thing is for sure, I love you with faith.
And if my faith gets weak, I'll love you with grace.

A Letter from an American

As I woke up, smelling the warm cappuccino scent coming from the Starbucks across the street, I see two individuals and they are telling me to leave the country. They are trying to take me to a country where I won't be able of watching the Yankees and the Red Sox go at it, or the Royals and Cardinals fight for state dominance. Where I won't be able to eat turkey at thanksgiving dinner and have a warm apple pie for dissert. They want me in a place where I won't be able of enjoying the presidential debate between the Republican and the Democrats during the election season. To a place where freedom can only be dreamed of and people are not equal in the eyes of justice. Where women are persecuted and have no one to stand up for them. A place where a college degree has no meaning and education is not valued at all. In a place where dreams are crushed and no one is given a chance. A place unlike the United State of America where freedom rings, where there is justice and equality for all.

"Take a look at me, am I really foreign?" I asked. "I eat American, I dress American, I drive American and I buy American. All I know is America. From the healthy sandwiches of subways to the fattening burgers and fries of McDonalds, I eat them all. With my levy's jean, my buckle belt and my Brooksbrothers jacket, I look no different from anyone else in America. I drive not a Honda, a Peugeot nor a Mercedes but a Lincoln. I'm a consumer of American made products, I love them all. I went to high school in this country; I became a man in this country; I got baptized in this nation. I learned to speak American since I never spoke a word of English when I first arrived in this blessed nation. Like Albert Gallatin, I'm also foreign born but dearly love America and feel American."

They still wouldn't listen to me, so I carried on. "I'm grateful to the founding fathers, and all that have died and are still dieing under the American flag as they fight for our liberties. Like Washington, I believe in the federal government. I have faith in the US constitution. I believe in the declaration of independence. I stand by the fourteenth amendment. I agree with Lincoln's Emancipation Proclamation and praise his Gettysburg Address. I pledge allegiance to the US flag and the republic for which it stands. Like Theodore Roosevelt, I believe in the diplomatic approach as we walk softly and carry a big stick. Like John F. Kennedy, I do not ask America what can it do for me, but rather ask myself what I can do for America. Like Rev. Martin Luther King Jr., I too have a dream. Like Reagan, I put my trust in the states of this city on the hill. Like Franklin D. Roosevelt, America has nothing to fear but fear itself, for this is the land of the free and the home of the brave. I support our troops in any battle they undertake no matter if I'm for or against the battle they are in. I support every American president no matter what their political affiliation may be. I believe in Democracy. I support the bipartisan approach to every decision that affects this nation. I cry when America cries and I laugh when America laughs, and as I believe in America, I too am an American, though I'm not a citizen." Then, they put chains on me and brought me where criminals are held. So now I cry with tears, and know that America cries with me.

Something to Think About (Quotes)

- "A long life is measured by how it was lived (by accomplishment) rather than years."

- "Searching for happiness is searching for a purpose, and that can only be found in Jesus Christ."

- "One can only meet destiny once one has met oneself."

- "Losing depends on one's understanding of wining."

- "It takes a humbler person to receive than give."

- "Failure is not to fail, but to give up."

- "Victory is to win or to lose without being defeated."

- "A million people can't do what one man can do if one man can do what takes a million people to do."

- "No one gets to heaven until one leaves the earth."

- "Nothing gets down from heaven until something goes up from the earth."

- "Mocking one's mistake is mocking our humanity."

- "Living happily is not so much living with pleasures but rather with satisfactions."

- "Going home is going where one 's own state of mind is at peace (ease)"

- "We only miss the things or people that we are dearly attached to consciously or subconsciously."

- Knowledge does bring power, but with it comes the risk of propaganda as it infiltrates a hidden agenda in people's mind.

- "Pennies from heaven are millions on earth; millions on earth are not worth a penny in heaven."

CPSIA information can be obtained at www.ICGtesting.com
Printed in the USA
BVOW02s1004110216

436366BV00001B/58/P